MW01280096

The technical stuff:
Walk written and published by Joel Nagel
Cover Art by Neville McKinnie
More resources available at www.lansingchurch.org

Walk

"So I say, walk by the Spirit, and you will not gratify the desires of the flesh...Since we live by the Spirit, let us keep in step with the Spirit."

-GALATIANS 5:16, 25

Building close relationships with people can be challenging enough. Building a deep relationship with an invisible, all-powerful God can seem impossible at times. Many Christians have a hard time connecting with God, simply because they don't know how to have meaningful devotional times. Just as communication is the key to any human relationship, communication is the key to a great relationship with God.

God has done his part to start a conversation with us by writing a timeless and perfect book that tells his story. When we read the bible we are sitting down and listening to the very words of God as inspired by the Spirit. Good communication goes both ways. It is essential that we learn to love listening to God's word but he also wants to hear from us. This is where prayer comes in. Often reading and prayer are seen as separate parts of one's relationship with God. But prayerful reading can turn up the volume on anyone's quiet time.

This journal is a conversation starter with God. As you begin listening to his word and responding through prayer, you will get to know God through his story and see your place in the story as well.

Are you ready to walk by the Spirit?

Contents Check List

(Cross off as you complete each study and section)

1. The Law, Old and New

    1.1. Genesis 1

    1.2. John 1, Colossians 1, Revelation 21

    1.3. Genesis 2-3

    1.4. Romans 5-6

    1.5. Genesis 12, 21-22

    1.6. John 8, Galatians 3-4

    1.7. Exodus 32-34

    1.8. Hebrews 3-4

    1.9. Deuteronomy 5-6

    1.10. Matthew 5-7

Meet up to review with your Discipleship Partner

2. OT History, NT History

    2.1. Joshua 6-7

    2.2. Matthew 18, Acts 5

    2.3. Judges 2-3

    2.4. John 16-17

    2.5. 1 Samuel 16-17

    2.6. Acts 9, 2 Corinthians 12

2.7. 1 Kings 9-10

2.8. Acts 8, 1 Peter 5

2.9. 2 Kings 17, 2 Chronicles 36

2.10. Acts 1-2

Meet up to review with your Discipleship Partner

3. Poetry and Prophecy

   3.1. Job 1, 38, 42

   3.2. Psalm 19, Romans 1

   3.3. Psalm 133, 1 Corinthians 3

   3.4. Psalm 22, Matthew 27

   3.5. Isaiah 52-53, Luke 23-24

   3.6. Jeremiah 1, Ezekiel 2

   3.7. Daniel 2, Matthew 1-2

   3.8. Hosea 1-2, 1 Peter 2

   3.9. Haggai 1, Acts 4-5

   3.10. Malachi 4, Matthew 3

Meet up to review with your Discipleship Partner

4. Gospel

   4.1. John 1-2

   4.2. John 3-4

   4.3. John 5-6

4.4. John 7-8

4.5. John 9-10

4.6. John 11-12

4.7. John 13-14

4.8. John 15-17

4.9. John 18-19

4.10. John 20-21

Meet up to review with your Discipleship Partner

5. <u>Letters</u>

5.1. Romans 7-8

5.2. 2 Corinthians 4-5

5.3. Ephesians 4-6

5.4. Philippians 2-4

5.5. 1 Thessalonians 1, 5

5.6. 1 Timothy 3-4

5.7. Hebrews 11-12

5.8. James 1-2

5.9. 1 John 2, 4

5.10. Revelation 2-3

Meet up to review with your Discipleship Partner

Before the journey begins…

Learn how to walk through the word of God.

The SOAP Method of Prayerful Reading

Many people struggle with taking notes while reading the bible, but taking notes is essential for those who really want to grow in Christ. A lot of the problems with taking notes come down to not having a notebook and not knowing what to write. This journal takes care of both of those issues. All you need is a bible and a pen!

When you read each passage take notes using the S.O.A.P method. S.O.A.P stands for Scripture, Observation, Application and Prayer. Let's break it down further:

- **Scripture:** The most important part of any devotional time is the scripture you read. Read carefully. Read out loud if possible. Read confusing parts again. This isn't about getting a reading time in. It's about connecting with God.

- **Observation:** As you read, take notes on anything that is interesting to you. Write down key passages. Write down any questions you may have. Don't be afraid to do a little research on the internet or with resources you have. Look up words. Write down similar passages that come to mind as you build your knowledge of the bible.

- **Application:** Observation without application can cause us to become puffed up by knowledge without gaining true wisdom. Look over your notes and observations. How can you apply what you read to your day? Is there some way that your character needs to change? Try to think of practical ways that you could turn a lesson from the passage into a reality in your life.

- **Prayer:** This is the other side of the conversation. Do you see how a thorough reading with thoughtful observation and humble application will give you a lot to talk to God about? Ask him your questions. Talk to him about how to apply the passage to your life.

You still might not have a life changing devotional time every day, but over time you should be able to fall deeply in love with God by committing to daily conversations such as these.

A Journey Through God's Story

A seemingly small thing that frequently keeps people from consistent and meaningful times with God is simply not knowing what to read. The passages in this journal have been chosen to give new disciples an overview of the story of God. God's word is not a typical book. It is filled with different styles of writing or genres. Just as you'd be pretty disappointed if you went to go see a romantic comedy and ended up in a horror movie, reading parts of the bible with little knowledge of the genre can lead to confusion instead of inspiration. Each of the 5 sections is given a brief introduction and each passage is also introduced to help you understand context and make connections.

As we look at the individual genres it is also important to see how they fit together to become one amazing story of creation, rebellion and redemption. Thus, the Old Testament readings are supplemented by complimentary readings from the New Testament. The goal is to give new disciples a foundation from which to dive deeper into God's word.

A People of the Word

One of the best features of coming to Christ through bible study is the interaction you get to have with other disciples. Many new disciples have desired more one-on-one bible studies, especially right after their conversion. Indeed, our conversations with each other are an essential part of our conversation with God. After all, he came to give us a kingdom and a family as well as personal salvation.

In order to further develop your relationships in the church there is a discipleship time at the end of each section. As you complete the devotional times for each section, set up a time to meet with your discipleship partner, house church leader or the person who studied the bible with you. These devotionals are designed to take the conversation you've been having with God into the church. Who knows the impact your times with God will have as you discuss your observations, questions and applications with a trusted friend. The Great Commission (Matthew 28:18-20) tells us to "Go and make disciples" *and* to "teach them everything commanded." It is the goal of this booklet that every disciple complete all 5 sections and all 5 discipleship times as a way of beginning to fulfill both parts of Jesus' last command.

Section 1: The Law, Old and New

Let's start in the beginning.

Many people have a negative reaction to laws and law enforcement. We want our freedom! But the bible teaches us the value of law. In the Old Testament, the Law of Moses consists of the first 5 books of the bible. Some of the laws may seem restrictive or strange but if we consider the needs of Israel during the time of Moses the laws make sense.

Israel had been enslaved for 400 years in Egypt. God miraculously rescued them through plagues on Egypt and the crossing of the sea. Because of sin, they had to stay in the desert for 40 years before they could enter the Promised Land and become the nation of Israel. Here's where the laws come in: How can a brand new nation exist without laws to govern it? How can a people claim a nationality without knowing their common origins? Thus, the first books of the bible are filled with the laws and origins of Israel, the special people of God.

The readings in this first section are not just focused on the Law of Moses. The New Testament emphasizes freedom but Jesus also promises that the law will not pass away (Matthew 5:17). Indeed, as God's people we are a part of his kingdom and under the law of that kingdom. In order to see how the Old Testament law and the promises of the New Testament work together, these readings go back and forth from old to new. As you read, look for ways that the old law and new law overlap. Instead of cancelling the old law, the New Testament enhances the old, creating a law of grace through the work of Jesus Christ.

The legal requirements may have changed but the heart of God and the hearts of people remain the same. God's law, old and new, serves as a safety net for his people, that they may be blessed through faithful obedience.

1.1 The Beginning

Genesis 1 is a story of origins. Theologians, scientists, skeptics and people of faith all read this chapter and come to different conclusions. The fact that people are looking for conclusions may be why it is such a controversial passage. Instead of coming to conclusions, we should remember that this is quite literally the beginning. This passage should open our minds instead of closing them. As you read, look for eternal truths. Listen to the poetry. Thank God for creating something amazing and for creating you to be a part of it.

SOAP: Genesis 1

1.2 A New Beginning

It's hard to imagine anything trumping the creation of the universe but as we read through the bible we see that God's creation went beyond the physical universe. Through Christ, God did more than just create. He created a way for each of us to have a new beginning.

SOAP: John 1, Colossians 1:15-23, Revelation 21:1-7

1.3 The Fall

The bible doesn't shy away from life's big questions. Right after proclaiming God as the creator, Genesis answers the question, "Why is the world so messed up?" The answer is because of us. From the very beginning we brought sin into the world. It is our nature to rebel against God. Today's reading may not seem like a law but it's really the story of the law that governs our world to this day: where there is sin, there is death.

SOAP: Genesis 2-3

1.4 The Law of Grace

In Christ, we have the answer to sin and death. But we still live in a world that is full of sin. We are surrounded by temptations that will result in slavery and darkness. Everyone is a slave to something. As Christians we must choose to be slaves to Christ and in doing so become truly free.

SOAP: Romans 5-6

1.5 Calling, Promise and Testing

After the stories of origins in Genesis, we get to see God's plan to save his people start to unfold. His plan begins with a family struggling to have a child. Abraham desperately desires to be a father, but God has a plan for him to be the father of an entire nation and for his bloodline to run through Jesus himself someday. But first he has to believe in the promise of God and pass an incredible test.

SOAP: Genesis 12:1-9, 21-22

1.6 Promise Fulfilled

Abraham never got to see God's promise fulfilled in his lifetime. In fact, it took hundreds of years for God to use Abraham's family to become a blessing to all. But God kept his promise and he did it in the most unexpected way. Today's chapters feature Jesus bluntly explaining the promise of Abraham to the Jewish leaders of his day and Paul tying Abraham's promise into Christian theology.

SOAP: John 8, Galatians 3:1-4:7

1.7 The Mountain of God

As Moses receives the law from God on Mount Sinai, the people below descend into chaos and idolatry. These chapters are a great reminder that we are never far from mountain top experiences with God. But at the same time, we are never far from forgetting about God and going our own way.

SOAP: Exodus 32-34

1.8 Rebellion in the Desert

Israel's rebellious ways continued throughout their wanderings in the desert. The New Testament author of Hebrews weighs in on the spiritual lessons we can learn from the desert generation as we seek to enter his rest on that Day.

SOAP: Hebrews 3-4

1.9 The Heart Of The Law

Deuteronomy literally means "second giving of the law". Moses gets one last chance to lead his people before they enter the Promised Land after spending 40 years in the desert. The presentation of the law that he gives gets to the heart and purpose of the law for Israel. What timeless truths can you find and apply to your life?

SOAP: Deuteronomy 5-6

1.10 The Law of The Kingdom

The Sermon on the Mount is the longest continuous teaching by Jesus in the bible. The mountain setting should remind us of Moses' law that was given from a mountain. Christ's law for his soon to come Kingdom is just as challenging and essential as the Law of Moses. What challenges you the most?

SOAP: Matthew 5-7

Discipleship Time 1: The Law, Old and New

Meet up with your discipleship partner and bring him or her into your conversation with God.

1. Looking over your notes, which passage did you find the most interesting? Why?

2. What will be the most challenging lesson to apply to your life? Discuss ways that you can live out the scriptures with your study partner.

3. Looking back at your conversion, how has Jesus used his power to create a new life for you?

4. Is there any sin that you are still enslaved by? Is there any temptation that you have found difficult to face? Have a time of open and honest discussion.

5. In your time with our church have you discovered any ways that God may be calling you to serve or have impact? Talk about ideas with your study partner.

6. Can you think of any ways that the lessons you've learned about God's law could help people around you? Is there a family member, co-worker or friend that would benefit from hearing about what your learning? Talk with your study partner about how to approach the people you care about with the love of God.

7. Perhaps the most challenging part of this section is the last reading from the Sermon on the Mount. What part of Christ's law did you find the most challenging? How can you start following the king's rule?

End your time together by looking ahead at the next section and praying about the things you discussed.

Section 2: OT History, NT History

The God of the bible has often been called "the God of history". This doesn't mean that he is boring like your high school history class or that he is ancient history that is no longer relevant. It means that he has shaped human history by inserting his presence at key moments. Far from being ancient history, he is still active in the events of our world and our lives.

God's work in our world is evidenced throughout the bible but particularly in the historical writings of the Old and New Testament. In the Old Testament, the historical writings pick up right where Moses left off. Joshua tells the story of Israel's conquest of the Promised Land. Judges and Samuel tell the story of how Israel became a kingdom. Kings and Chronicles tell the story of Israel's kings, division and destruction. Over the course of hundreds of years of ups and downs, faithfulness and apostasy, we see that God never abandons his people.

The New Testament has only one book of history: the book of Acts. It continues the story of God's kingdom but at the head of this new kingdom is Jesus himself. This is the same kingdom that we are citizens of to this day through the church. We get glimpses of this kingdom in other parts of the New Testament that we will look at as well.

Like the last section, these readings go back and forth from old to new to show the consistency of God's eternal story and to help us apply the stories of the old kingdom to our lives as members of his everlasting kingdom. As you SOAP these passages look for ways to apply the lessons of the kingdom to your kingdom life today.

2.1 The Walls of Jericho

By the end of the book of Joshua, Israel will have defeated 31 city-states in the Promised Land between the Jordan River and the Mediterranean Sea. The greatest challenge they faced in their conquest wasn't the army of Jericho but obedience to God.

SOAP: Joshua 6-7

2.2 Breaking Down Walls in the Church

It may be shocking that God is willing to use the death penalty in the New Testament. His standard of righteousness does not change. To protect his kingdom in its infancy, God goes to great lengths to ensure that Christ's teaching about his church is taken seriously.

SOAP: Matthew 18:1-20, Acts 5:1-11

2.3 Cycles of Rebellion, Desperation and Salvation

The book of Judges introduces us to an all too familiar cycle in which nations and individuals alike often find themselves. First, comes rebellion. With rebellion from God come consequences, little morsels of wrath to keep us from losing God completely. After a miserable period of tasting God's wrath for our rebellion we wake up and desperately call upon God. When we call upon him, he leads us to salvation. "Judge" means leader in Hebrew. The judges were the people that God appointed to save Israel every time they repented from their rebellion.

SOAP: Judges 2:6-3:6

2.4 Led By The Spirit

The cycle of rebellion, desperation and salvation is still active in our world today. Through Christ, we have the ultimate judge leading us to salvation: The Holy Spirit. As mysterious as he may be, the Spirit is our greatest resource when we are tempted to rebel. He pleads with God on our behalf when we are desperate and he seals our salvation as he answers Jesus' prayer for the unity of his people.

SOAP: John 16, Galatians 5

2.5 The Making of a King After God's Own Heart

Meet David, the shepherd, harpist, giant slayer and king that set the standard for all kings to come. In these chapters we get a glimpse of the humility and passion that made him capable of leading God's people.

SOAP: 1 Samuel 16-17

2.6 The Greatest Apostle

From the greatest king to the greatest apostle: Paul. Today we'll look at two of the moments when Christ spoke to Paul. First, we'll see his calling and conversion on the road to Damascus. Then, we'll read about a lesson he learned through the trials of living for God alone.

SOAP: Acts 9:1-19, 2 Corinthians 12:1-10

2.7 The Wisest King?

Solomon's story is both great and terrible. On the one hand, his Godly wisdom allowed Israel to expand and grow more wealthy and influential than any other time in its history. But on the other hand, his misuse of God's gifts and pride ultimately lead to the kingdom being divided under the rule of his son. What lessons can you glean from Solomon's life?

SOAP: 1 Kings 9-10

2.8   Growing and Protecting God's Kingdom

The kingdom of God is supposed to grow and multiply. In today's reading we see how God can grow his church from the most unlikely circumstances. As the church grows, however, it faces internal and external threats.

SOAP: Acts 8, 1 Peter 5:1-11

2.9 How The Kingdom Crumbles

Solomon's son caused the kingdom of Israel to be split in two: Israel in the North and Judah in the south. Today we will look at the fall and exile of both of those kingdoms. Israel fell to Assyria in 722 BC. Judah was exiled to Babylon in 586 BC. Look for similarities and even grace as you read the sad ending of these nations that were supposed to hold God's standard.

SOAP: 2 Kings 17, 2 Chronicles 36:15-23

2.10 The Coming of The Kingdom

God may have allowed his people to go into exile but he never abandoned them. In fact, after bringing them back from exile, the God of history worked his plan to insert himself into our history like never before. He lived and died as one of us. And then, having conquered death he left behind his new kingdom. Today's reading tells of the kingdom's inaugural day!

SOAP: Acts 1-2

Discipleship Time 2: OT History, NT History

Meet up with your discipleship partner and bring him or her into your conversation with God.

1. Looking over your notes, which passage did you find the most interesting? Why?

2. What will be the most challenging lesson to apply to your life? Discuss ways that you can live out the scriptures with your study partner.

3. These passages focus on God's kingdom. Can you think of any lessons from your reading or notes that will help you be a greater citizen of God's kingdom?

4. Have you found yourself stuck in any cycles since coming to God? How can you stay rooted in Christ and grow out of any harmful cycles?

5. Pride and disunity were threats to God's kingdom in the Old Testament that still threaten to tear apart his kingdom today. Can you think of any instances where you've been tempted with pride or disunity?

6. Because Christ's church is built on deep relationships there are bound to be disagreements. Can you think of anything from these passages that will help you when conflict arises?

7. Take a moment to discuss God's history with your bible study partner. You are a part of a grand history that spans centuries as well as a personal history that mirrors Acts 1-2. The God of history not only breaks into the events of our world to see his will done, he also breaks into our lives that we may have the opportunity to live for him. Discuss this with one another and praise God!

End your time together by looking at the next section of readings and praying.

Section 3: Poetry and Prophecy

In this section we will examine two closely related genres in scripture. Poetry and Prophecy make the bible come to life and teach us that God cares not just about our actions but about our hearts and motives. Indeed, the longest book at the very center of the bible is a book of poetry. That speaks loudly about the heart of God.

Hebrew poetry and prophecy are linked by style and substance. The style of both is poetic but not like a modern rhyming poem or song that we may be used to. Hebrew poetic form is called parallelism. Instead of rhyming word sound, Hebrew poetry rhymes ideas by expressing an idea in one line and then magnifying it or contrasting it with the next line. Here is an example from Psalm 139: "You have searched me, Lord, and you know me." This is followed by the magnifying verse, "You know when I sit and when I rise; you perceive my thoughts from afar." The lines can also contrast each other with a similar effect as in Psalm 119:113, "I hate double-minded people, but I love your law." Much of the prophecy in the bible also follows this pattern of parallelism.

The substance of poetry and prophecy is also similar. It is hard to shake the false image of prophecy that many have. Prophets were not future predictors as much as they were present proclaimers. Instead of looking forward and telling of disaster they actually looked back at the law of God with its blessings and curses and then looked at the present state of God's people and pronounced judgment. In some of those judgments, God used the prophets to dream about grander future plans to deliver mankind once and for all through the messiah. We find prophecies about the messiah and God's coming kingdom in the books of prophecy as well as the books of poetry. In fact, after Isaiah, Psalms is the most often quoted book in the New Testament.

To help you build connections between the prophecies of the Old Testament and their fulfillment in the New Testament, this section provides readings from Old and New. May you marvel at God's power and love as you see his plan foretold and realized over many generations and even today!

3.1 The Saga of Job

Job is a hard read about an even harder life. The sovereignty of God is boldly proclaimed from start to finish in Job's story. The middle sections that are not included in this reading tell the story of Job's "friends" who doubt his righteousness and blame him for his calamity. In all of his suffering and ridicule, Job holds on to his trust in God even if only by a thread.

SOAP: Job 1, 38, 42 (all of 38-42 if possible)

3.2 God's Revelation of Himself Leaves Us With No Excuse

This Psalm teaches us two ways that God reveals himself to us. First, there is general revelation. The sky, the sun, the universe and all of creation speak to the existence of a creator. But beyond that God has given us what theologians call "special" revelation though his word. In case creation wasn't enough he wrote us an incredible book. In Romans 1, Paul teaches us the implications of living in a world in which God has clearly revealed himself to all.

SOAP: Psalm 19, Romans 1

3.3 The Importance of Unity

The Old and New Testaments are unified about the importance of unity. Psalm 133 is in a section of Psalms called the Songs Of Ascents that were sung as pilgrims made their way to Jerusalem for festivals. How important unity must have been for the people coming together to worship as one in Jerusalem. The entire context of Paul's first letter to the church in Corinth is the disunity that the church was suffering.

SOAP: Psalm 133, 1 Corinthians 3

3.4 Forsaken

Jesus' cry from the cross in Aramaic, "Eli, Eli, lema sabachthani" even caused confusion for the people who stood at the foot of the cross. They wondered if he was calling Elijah. In the centuries that have followed, theologians have debated other aspects of this passage such as whether or not Jesus was actually separated from God. If we keep in mind that Jesus was quoting David's Psalm 22 we can gain great insight into the cry of Christ from the cross.

SOAP: Psalm 22, Matthew 27

3.5 The Suffering Servant

The second half of Isaiah is composed of prophecies that center around the coming of the messiah or chosen savior. Isaiah spoke these words some 700 years before Christ and the Dead Sea Scrolls contain a copy of Isaiah that dates before Jesus lived. May your faith be bolstered and challenged by today's reading.

SOAP: Isaiah 52:13-53:12, Luke 23-24

3.6 Calling

As we shift from poetry to prophecy we get to see one of the distinct features of prophecy: the prophetic call. A true prophet spoke the very words of God after responding to God's call with humility. As we read, we can consider the callings that God has given us and the inevitable opposition that comes to those who are called.

SOAP: Jeremiah 1, Ezekiel 2, Luke 19:1-10

3.7 Kingdom Come

Daniel's interpretation of the king's dream is one of the most amazing prophecies of the bible. The layers of the statue represent the empires that will come before God establishes his eternal kingdom. When the messiah finally comes he is nothing like the militaristic king that so many expected. Jesus comes as the humblest of kings.

SOAP: Daniel 2, Matthew 1-2

3.8 Unending Love

After spending time in exile, God graciously allows his people to come back and re-establish themselves in the Promised Land. *Hesed* is the Hebrew word for unconditional love that today's reading illustrates. We may separate ourselves from God and fail our side of the covenant but God always finds a way to take our brokenness and make for himself a people.

SOAP: Hosea 1-2, 1 Peter 2

3.9 Building Up The Kingdom

After returning from exile, the Israelites had the difficult task of rebuilding Jerusalem and the temple. They may have given up if it weren't for the creative rebuke of Haggai. Similarly, the early church faced internal challenges that could have ceased it from being built up.

SOAP: Haggai 1, Acts 4:32-5:11

3.10 One Last Preview

Our Old Testament ends with one last preview of what the kingdom will be like when it comes. We are told that the great prophet Elijah will come to pave the way for the messiah. Jesus himself proclaims this prophecy fulfilled in the life of one of the bible's great heroes: John the Baptist.

SOAP: Malachi 4, Matthew 3

Discipleship Time 3: Poetry and Prophecy

Meet up with your discipleship partner and bring him or her into your conversation with God.

1. Looking over your notes, which passage did you find the most interesting? Why?

2. What will be the most challenging lesson to apply to your life? Discuss ways that you can live out the scriptures with your study partner.

3. How has God revealed himself to you through his creation, through trials and joys in your life, and through his word?

4. Take some time to revisit Christ's passion (suffering) that you read through in this section. How does it make you feel that God planned so much pain for his son so that we could be healed?

5. As a disciple, you have been called. And just like the prophets we often face stubborn people. How should people's responses affect our mission to save the world?

6. Have you been building up God's kingdom or building up your own life more? In what ways can you focus more on building the kingdom for Christ?

7. Is there anyone in your life that is not a part of God's people? God has not abandoned them! In fact, you may be God's answer to their need for him. Talk with your discipleship partner about who you could reach and how.

End your time together by talking about any needs you have, being open and praying for the kingdom to come to the lost all around us!

Section 4: Gospel

The gospel (or good news) in the bible comes to us in the 4 books that begin the New Testament. Matthew, Mark, Luke and John do not attempt to tell us the whole story of Jesus' life. If that was their goal they missed large parts. Instead of being a biography, a gospel is a pointed and purposeful presentation of Jesus Christ as the messiah to come. The writers are biased. They believe that Jesus was the Son of God and they want you to believe it too! So they chose stories and lessons from the life of Jesus that would prove Jesus to those who didn't believe and inspire those who believed already. May you be inspired as you read the good news of God that came in the life, death and resurrection of Jesus Christ.

The first three gospels, Matthew, Mark and Luke are called "synoptic" because they look alike. They borrowed from the same sources and even from each other to tell three unique but similar stories of the Messiah. The fourth gospel, written by the apostle John, is very different. He probably wrote his gospel after the others were in circulation among the early churches so his gospel purposely takes a different approach. More than the first three gospels, the gospel of John focuses on the words of Jesus. From the first verse we know that this will be the focus as he re-writes Genesis 1:1 saying that, "In the beginning was the Word, and the Word was with God, and the Word was God." The Word is Jesus himself and his words are the star of this gospel.

The first generation of Christians had no biblical writing besides the Old Testament. Instead, they had the apostles who had been with Jesus to tell the story of his life. An apostle would travel from church to church teaching about Jesus. The gospel of John is our chance to sit at the feet of the early Christians and hear what John, Jesus' beloved disciple, would teach when he went from church to church. Without the bible, a visit from an apostle must have been an amazing occasion. You can imagine a house packed with people wanting to hear John speak about his friend Jesus. When we read the gospel of John, we get to have that same experience. Let's approach these readings with the same enthusiasm that our ancient brothers and sisters must have had no matter how many times we've heard John's words.

4.1 The Light Dawns

John skips the birth and childhood stories that other gospels include and goes much farther back. He establishes that Jesus was with God and active from the very beginning. These chapters also show the beginnings of Jesus' ministry as he calls his first disciples and reluctantly performs his first miracle. Keep in mind the readings you've done from the Old Testament and look for powerful connections.

SOAP: John 1-2

4.2 Living Water

Jesus ministers to Nicodemus and lays out his teaching that includes belief, repentance and baptism. Can you find all three in Jesus' nighttime conversation? Later he meets with a foreign woman and teaches her about living water and true worship.

SOAP: John 3-4

4.3 Eat Jesus

Whenever Jesus performs a miracle it is for the purpose of highlighting his teaching. Can you imagine being in the crowd and hearing Jesus proclaim that we need to eat his flesh? It's not surprising that the crowd gets a lot smaller after Jesus' teaching. This is a good reminder that Jesus doesn't lower his standard to include everyone. We have to live up to his standards if we want to separate ourselves from the crowd and remain disciples.

SOAP: John 5-6

4.4 Children of Abraham

From the very beginning, God has worked through one chosen family or people to show the world what it means to be righteous and receive salvation. You've read about this special line when you read about Adam and Eve, Abraham and David, and many others. With each chosen family comes a rejected family. In these chapters Jesus reveals to the Jewish leaders that they are no longer God's chosen people. God's favor now rests with Christ's people - but they are welcome to join!

SOAP: John 7-8

4.5 Blind Guides

Today we see an epic encounter between Jesus and the Jewish leaders over the healing of a man born blind. He uses the healing and the drama surrounding it to show everyone that the truly blind people are the leaders themselves. Then he proclaims himself to be the true guide and shepherd for Israel's lost sheep.

SOAP: John 9-10

4.6 Raising The Dead

John foreshadows Jesus' resurrection by showing the power of God to raise a dead man named Lazarus. We get to see Jesus' compassion and his power as he calls to the dead man and he stumbles out of the tomb. As Jesus enters Jerusalem in a kingly procession, he contrasts his coronation by predicting his own impending death.

SOAP: John 11-12

4.7 An Unforgettable Meal

Before Jesus is arrested and killed, he spends a most special evening eating with his disciples and teaching them. What would you do if you only had one night to live? Jesus spends special time with his friends. He starts by humbly washing their feet and then he reminds them of his most important teachings.

SOAP: John 13-14

4.8 Last Words

Jesus concludes his upper room discourse by explaining the role of the Holy Spirit, inevitable persecution and the importance of staying deeply connected to God. The longest prayer that we have from Jesus has one focus: Unity.

SOAP: John 15-17

4.9 The Death of Jesus

The intimacy of the last supper is interrupted by Judas' betrayal and the disciples' denial. Jesus dies like the humble king that he had shown the world throughout his life. If we read these chapters with humility we can see ourselves in the people who interacted with the cross. Indeed, we have all been denying disciples, faithless Pharisees and mindless mobs in our sin.

SOAP: John 18-19

4.10 You Can't Keep a God-Man Down

This wouldn't be good news without these chapters. Many of us have become desensitized to how amazing this really is because we've heard it all our lives. Try to read it again for the first time. Jesus rose from the dead! He spends his last days on earth getting the disciples ready to build his church.

SOAP: John 20-21

Discipleship Time 4: Gospel

Meet up with your discipleship partner and bring him or her into your conversation with God.

1. Looking over your notes, which passage did you find the most interesting? Why?

2. What will be the most challenging lesson to apply to your life? Discuss ways that you can live out the scriptures with your study partner.

3. John constantly presents Jesus as one who is totally tied into his relationship with God. How close are you to God? How reliant?

4. Our spiritual diet affects our relationship with God and with other people just like our diet effects our health. Besides eating Jesus and drinking living water, are you putting other things in your life that may be hurting your spiritual health?

5. Talk about blindness. Are there any blind spots in your character or walk with God that your discipleship partner could help reveal?

6. Jesus sets an amazing example of servitude and submission when he washes his disciples feet. Can you think of any ways that you could serve others in a greater way?

7. In the end, Jesus reinstates Peter at the "first breakfast". Are there any relationship issues in your life or in the church that need resolved? Do you need to forgive anyone? Use your discipleship partner as a sounding board for advice.

End your time together by looking at the next section of readings and praying.

Section 5: Letters

Letters ("epistles" in Greek) are a significant genre in the New Testament. Learning spiritual lessons from the letters is all about context. Here's an example of the importance of context: Imagine finding a letter on the ground. In order to figure out who wrote the message and who it was written for, you have to do some digging. You have to try and find out who wrote it and what they were originally responding to. What is the occasion of the letter? You can look for clues in the text, names, locations and events. From that one correspondence you can learn a lot.

The letters of the New Testament are like this. We have a letter written by someone to someone else or to a church. Using clues within the letter we can determine who wrote it, who it was written to, and why they wrote it. Once we know the context we can learn from the letter without dangerously pulling verses out of context. Before you read a letter it is good to use a commentary, a bible handbook or the introduction to each book found in a study bible to figure out the context. As we look through key passages in the letter, each reading will be introduced with enough context to get the big picture.

The letters of the New Testament are an amazing gift to the church. We get to hear first hand accounts of what life in the early church was like. The wisdom passed on to each church or individual served the original audience but the Holy Spirit has made these correspondences timeless and enduringly relevant. Finding practical applications for your life should not be difficult. You'll see that although many things have changed in the 2,000 years since Christ came, our hearts and our struggles remain the same. Thus, the answers given to the early Christians in the first churches still cut our hearts and heal our souls to this day.

As with the rest of this journal, the readings have been kept to 2-3 chapters to keep from overwhelming anyone. But, if you are able, please read the smaller letters in their entirety. After all, who only reads the first and last paragraph of their emails?

5.1 More Than Conquerors

Paul's letter to the Romans is one coherent argument explaining sin, grace and redemption to the Roman church to ready them for a visit he hoped to make. These chapters hone in on the amazing grace of God. Rome needed this teaching because people were coming to the church and falsely teaching that in order to become a Christian you had to be Jewish first and follow all of the Old Testament laws. As we've seen in previous readings, the Old Testament law is fulfilled in Christ. His interpretation of the law is the only law we need and his death and resurrection give us the new life that the Old law could never deliver.

SOAP: Romans 7-8

5.2 Jars of Clay

Paul's first letter to the church in Corinth was a brutal rebuke of their disunity and gross sin. It's strangely encouraging to know that the early church was far from perfect. Corinth had major issues but Corinth also had major repentance! Paul's second letter is in response to that repentance. These chapters remind us that any hardship that we face in this life will not last forever. In fact, Jesus has taken the worst that this world has to offer so that the only thing that will last forever is our eternity with him.

SOAP: 2 Corinthians 4-5

5.3 The Armor of God

Paul's letter to the church in Ephesus (present day Turkey) is full of encouragement. Today's chapters are some of the most practical chapters on Christian living in the whole bible. Look for Paul's instructions for the church, leadership, marriage, parenting and work life.

SOAP: Ephesians 4-6

5.4 Have The Same Mindset As Christ Jesus

Paul wrote this letter, which has the word "joy" in it more than any other New Testament work from a prison cell. What a testament to the power of Christ to bring peace in all circumstances. The poem in 2:5-11 is called the "kenosis hymn". Kenosis is the Greek word for empty. The song teaches us how Christ emptied himself of all of his God-ness so that we could be saved. Many Christians have found this to be their favorite book in the bible.

SOAP: Philippians 2, 4 (Read the whole letter if you can!)

5.5 Your Faith In God Has Become Known Everywhere

Paul's letters to the Thessalonian Church have more biblical context than any other letter. The story of the church's rough planting can be found in Acts 17:1-15 (go ahead and read it right now). As you can see, Paul had to leave the church in a hurry after only being there three weeks. They were not set up for success! Paul's letter is written in response to the good report Paul got from the infant church just a few months later. He praises God to discover that the poorly planted church is actually thriving.

SOAP: 1 Thessalonians 1, 5

5.6 Don't Let Anyone Look Down On You

Paul's letters were not just for churches. He also wrote to individuals such as ministers that he was training. In the letters to the young evangelists, Timothy and Titus, we get an inside look at leadership in the early church. In today's reading we learn the requirements for eldership (a noble task!) and the teaching that good leaders give to their churches.

SOAP: 1 Timothy 3-4

5.7 The Hall Of Fame Of Faith

The author of the letter to the Hebrews is one of the bible's great mysteries. We know that it was written to disciples from a Jewish background but we do not know who wrote this amazing book. The letter is one big warning and encouragement to stay faithful and not give up. It links the Old and New Testament like no other book in the bible. Whoever wrote it was a biblical master with clear inspiration from the Holy Spirit!

SOAP: Hebrews 11-12

5.8 Do Not Merely Listen to The Word

James, the (half) brother of Jesus became the leader of the early church in Jerusalem. Like the other general epistles that follow the book of Hebrews, the letter is named after its author (unlike Paul's letters which are named after the recipients of the letter). James' work has caused a lot of controversy over the years. Martin Luther famously called it a "gospel of straw" and wanted it removed from the bible. James will always be a thorn to those who wish to cheapen grace by separating what we do from what we believe.

SOAP: James 1-2 (Read the whole book if you can!)

5.9 God Is Love

John's first letter is filled with lessons about two seemingly opposite forces: love and judgment. Thus, reading this letter causes many to feel totally encouraged and a little insecure at the same time. When we accept John's picture of who God is this makes sense. He loves us with an eternal love but he is also going to be our eternal judge. He is merciful and just. Praise God that John, the beloved disciple of Jesus, was able to teach us what being with Jesus taught him about the unfathomable character of God.

SOAP: 1 John 2, 4 (You can read it all!)

5.10 You Have Forsaken The Love You Had At First

The bible ends with an amazingly encouraging book written by John to churches that were suffering persecution. Although many have misused this letter for personal profit, we should not be afraid of reading and being inspired by God's last word in the Word. The most accessible section contains 7 letters written to churches that John oversaw even as he was imprisoned. Our church can learn so much from the strengths and weaknesses of these churches.

SOAP: Revelation 2-3

Discipleship Time 5: Letters

Meet up with your discipleship partner and bring him or her into your conversation with God.

1. Looking over your notes, which passage did you find the most interesting? Why?

2. What will be the most challenging lesson to apply to your life? Discuss ways that you can live out the scriptures with your study partner.

3. Having read through parts of these letters, imagine if you were writing a letter to a fellow disciple. What would you tell him/her? If someone wrote a biblical letter to you what would you want to learn about?

4. Is there any sin that you are still enslaved to? Talk through ways that you can overcome and conquer with your discipleship partner.

5. Re-examine your notes from 1 Timothy 3 about being an elder. Is that something you desire? What characteristics are you missing and how could you begin growing into this honorable role?

6. Is there any area of your walk with God that is all talk but no walk? Talk about ways to turn your faith into practical action.

7. Look over your notes from Revelation 2-3. Did you identify with any of the encouragements or struggles that John wrote about to the 7 churches? Spend some time discussing.

Before you end in prayer, go over the next page together to make sure you are set up for great times with God now that you've finished this devotional journal.

Next

You did it! You've built a great foundation for your walk with God by spending 50 devotional times with Him! In the future, remember how helpful it is to have a plan for your devotional times. So many Christians drift from God simply because they lack a good plan. The old adage is certainly true here: If you fail to plan, you plan to fail.

There are many ways to read the bible and not get bored! No way is right or wrong. They all have different advantages depending on your learning style and what you want to learn. Here are a few ways to study the word:

Expositional: Reading a book of the bible from cover to cover is called expositional reading. The goal of such reading is to learn the lessons that were intended for the original audience and then to apply them to your life today. To do an expositional study, simply choose a book of the bible or a section of books and begin reading and taking notes just like you did in this journal. A *bible handbook* will greatly aid any expositional bible study.

Topical: Instead of reading a book of the bible and learning whatever lessons you come across, a topical study uses modern bible study tools (like a *concordance* or web search) to look at one concept throughout the bible. To begin, identify some things you would like to learn and create your own bible study on the topic. Some suggested topics are love, grace, justice, relationships, or any sin that you struggle with.

Character: Studying one of the bible's many colorful characters can be a great way to learn about our own character and grow in Christ. The bible is full of real men and women and it is brutally honest about their strengths and weaknesses. To study a biblical character choose someone you would like to learn about (i.e. David) and use a *concordance* to find out what books and chapters they are mentioned in. Many people are mentioned in places in the bible other than where their main story occurs. Be sure to check out those references as well.

Devotional: Many great books have been written about the books of the bible, the topics of the bible and the people of the bible. It is not recommended that you only read books about the bible and not the bible itself, but occasionally reading someone's take on the scriptures can be very encouraging and a great supplement to your own bible study. Ask a trusted friend for some book recommendations if you are looking for some inspiration. www.ipibooks.com is a great place to find books written by disciples for disciples.

One Last Thing

This journal was put together to help you have 50 great times with God. But the habits you built can help you have a lifetime of great times with God. Remember the simple things that you did to make these times great: Have a plan, read consistently, take notes, pray and share what you are learning with others. Here's to a SOAPy life!

Made in the USA
Las Vegas, NV
15 September 2021